CUT OFF THE EARS OF WINTER

New Issues Poetry & Prose

Editor	Herbert Scott
Copy Editor	Lisa Lishman
Managing Editor	Marianne Swierenga
Assistants to the Editor	Rebecca Beech, Christine Byks
Fiscal Officer	Marilyn Rowe

New Issues Poetry & Prose
The College of Arts and Sciences
Western Michigan University
Kalamazoo, MI 49008

First Edition, 2005.
Second printing, 2007.

ISBN	1-930974-50-7 (paperbound)
	1-930974-54-X (hardbound)

Library of Congress Cataloging-in-Publication Data:
Covino, Peter
Cut Off the Ears of Winter/Peter Covino
Library of Congress Control Number: 2004116688

Art Director	Tricia Hennessy
Designer	Vanessa Dickson
Production Manager	Paul Sizer
	The Design Center, Department of Art
	College of Fine Arts
	Western Michigan University

CUT OFF THE EARS OF WINTER

PETER COVINO

Dear Patrick!
With love
and admiration!
I'm insane!
xx Peter

New Issues

 WESTERN MICHIGAN UNIVERSITY

★ give the other book away!

for Edvige Giunta, sorella e sostegno;
and Agha Shahid Ali

Contents

III.

Acknowledgments

Thank you to the editors of the following publications where poems in this manuscript, sometimes in different versions, first appeared:

Art & Understanding: "Break"

Center for Book Arts (Broadside Series): "No Standing Still"

Cimarron Review: "Prescription," "Violence"

Columbia: "She Speaks to Me from the Birthing Waters"

Confrontation: "Caught"

Continuum (University of Utah): "Medicine of Language"

The Cortland Review: "At the *Museo Barberini*"

Evergreen Chronicles: "Dearest Evelyn, How Can I Make it Up to You?"

Italian Americana: "Lizard-Tree"

The Journal: "His Touch," "Midnight on the Fifth Day of a New Year"

The Metropolitan Review: "Now More Than Ever"

National Organization on Male Sexual Victimization Newsletter: "Sacrifice of Isaac"

New Orleans Review: "Pleiades"

Ohio Review: "Second Country"

The Paris Review: "At the Triple Treat Theatre"

Paterson Literary Review: "April 18th—Thinking About Lionel, Recently Dead of AIDS"

Poems & Plays: "An Offering"

Poet Lore: "The Way"

Rattapallax: "Promised Land"

Verse: "Cut Off the Ears of Winter"

Via: Voices in Italian Americana: "Picture Window," "Poverty of
  Language"

"At the Triple Treat Theatre" appeared in *This New Breed:
  Bad Boys, Gents and Barbarians 2:*, Rudy Kikel, Editor,
  Windstorm Creative, 2004.

"The Poverty of Language" was reprinted in *The Penguin
  Book of Italian American Writing*, Regina Barreca, Editor,
  Penguin, 2002.

Some of these poems first appeared in the chapbook, *Straight
Boyfriend,* winner of the 2001 Frank O'Hara Poetry Prize,
selected by Timothy Liu (Thorngate Road Press).

Special thanks to the University of Utah and the Ellen Christina
Steffensen Cannon family for a fellowship, the support of which
helped me to finish this book.

I would also like to thank Melissa Hotchkiss, Scott Hightower,
Phillis Levin, Lois Hirshkowitz, Mary Giaimo, Hollis Kurman,
Ellen Sobelman, Mary Cappello, Nancy Lipsitt, Ron Palmer,
Patricia Spears Jones, Daniela Gioseffi, Bob Viscusi, and
Kathleen Quinn for their unwavering support while I was
writing this book. Thank you also to my teachers Donald
Revell, Marilyn Hacker, Jacqueline Osherow, Karen Brennan,
Elaine Equi, and Martha Rhodes. Finally, abundant gratitude
to Herb Scott, Derek Pollard, and Lisa Lishman for making
this book possible and . . . especially Art.

Then said Jesus unto Peter, Put up thy sword . . .
—*John 18:10,11*

I.

Cut Off the Ears of Winter

Cut off the ears of winter
they have overheard too much,
where incinerators burn,
where rubble-strewn streets
are covered in dust from the remodeling.
Again, the doe-man in mauve cashmere—
the nerve of him—in the never world
(where ashes are harvested) where
ashes rain down in glory, a jackpot
of answers. Tonight, the underwriting
of desire is an inky carbon copy.
I *have* already—that last time drunk
on scotch. Then all morning
a chain gang of transvestite prostitutes
litters the front yard—the Police Station
next door also on fire, burning,
burning handcuffs, the soles of shoes
not holding the earth, cars skidding
everywhere, the tire's frame sets sparks
along the road. This is my last dollar,
last cigarette, last match.

TWO *from* PAST CHANNELS

ANTIGONE

Person of lips. Citizen
Of cosmos worthless
Except for the buzzing

Citizen of cosmos
I have been nowhere
No country no borders

Not enough earth
To bury me

JULIUS CAESAR

Like cherry wine, spilled sherry
Like the undergrowth of cotton
Replaced by Velcro. Innovation's

Plows roll you over.
Inside a field of wheat
Inside the sunburnt chaff.

The beer you are drinking
Mixed with lime.
Fusion of taste

Tipping the scales.
Veered back to the shaft.
Voice, a wind in fields

Small noise at night
Voice, a river lying down
Into itself

This burden I carry.
I sleep inside
The letter

Reducible to
A vacation in March.
A leopard.

Midnight on the Fifth Day of a New Year

Everyone is orange-tinted
or red-pink drear in those B-movies
from the '70s I can't cut off
at midnight on Channel 55.
Five days into the new year
and I'm wondering how much longer
it will be last year in my checkbook,
memos from work—the correspondence
piled higher on the lower left shelf.
Sweetie's swatting at a batch
destined for extinction,
rustling at my feet, his paw catches
my hand when I swish him away—
swish, the skin not breaking.
Michael Caine is the latest personality
disorder in this granular film
I've watched almost a half dozen times,
his hand keeps coming off every time
he's betrayed or angry, his hand
killing, mostly women who won't
love him back . . . and I'm feeling sorry
for the dying women, the hand he stabs
in one sequence, knife protruding.
Next, a bloodstained trail leads
to a deflated tire in a barn,
filmed from above, through hay,
wood beams. Now the expected turn:
this morbid fascination with dismemberment,
or why I can't cut off movies
about being buried alive;
in the muffled darkness,
a straw to breathe through
on a cold night in a new year.

April 18th—Thinking About Lionel, Recently Dead of AIDS

On this day, two days before he's to be selected in the NFL draft,
former Nebraska quarterback Brook Berringer is killed in a plane
     crash.

I'm reading this on my *Sports Illustrated* desktop calendar,
and last night I had trouble sleeping. I must have missed that
     story,

which is unusual since I love how the white noise of football
     reminds me of childhood,
and he almost made it to the pros. I'm thinking about almost
     making it:

why a drug addict sabotages himself by getting high the night
     before a drug test
or how on the anniversary of his sobriety the alcoholic gets wasted

at the Corner Saloon—I was there last week with Kate
and we shared two half-glasses of pale ale,

trying casually to understand again why her father left them
when she was eight, and he's holed up drunk

in some welfare hotel in Kentucky.
Because more is not what we're used to.

Like that made-for-cable-TV movie starring Anne Bancroft
as the lonely widow who suddenly finds herself raising four
     grandchildren.

I'm not paying close attention, because the caffeine's racing
     through me;
and last night at group we talked about how oversexualized we all
     feel:

kind of what Sr. Leanilda meant when she said St. Agatha felt blessed
when her captors hacked off her breasts—*an act of salvation from God.*

And one day, toward the end, Lionel called me into his office, which
    made me nervous
because he never did that, and he said not to live in fear like he has
    his whole life,

because sometimes when you take chances, you win.
And I can't help thinking what a fine name Brook Berringer is—

At the *Museo Barberini*

There are no others
in the painting,
only Judith and Holofernes,
and I am accustomed
to disappearing in allegory,

to hiding in the confines
of details. I am safer
here, standing in this gallery,
watching decapitations
and helplessness.

I will not be drawn in
by her billowing robes;
that wild mangle of folds
conceals a jagged sheath.
I have not yet mastered

the tricks of illusion;
perspective is always formed
at the vanishing point.
And I can be so easily betrayed:
she in all her fierce courage,

he of the familiar scowl—
these jealousies overwhelm me
at the most inopportune moments,
and I cannot say for sure
whose severed head she holds.

Second Country

By the time North Africa is annexed—
Ethiopia and Somalia, in quick succession—
he has already laid stake
to her genitalia.

Sometimes she savors the euphoria
of his drinking: he powerless, she sleeping
with the windows open—his crushed fedora,
broken crutches, the useless cobbler tools.

Just yesterday, it seems, over a wide expanse
of desert, he shot at defenseless men
wrapped in white cloth, carrying walking sticks—
toy soldiers.

Once, in a fit of desperation,
his wife shaved the side of her head
and mailed her hair along with a voided check
back to her brother in Venezuela.

Because she can no longer keep anything down,
he barters shoe repairs
and a silver cigarette case in exchange
for a ride into the city for medicine.

By mid-August, bright fireworks
saturate the skies of all the surrounding valleys
in spite of the Occupation
and lack of drinking water.

She imagines water splashing
into the fountain of the main piazza.
Her body—incense dissipating,
her breath fills the room.

In the Netherscape of That Earthquaked Town

—Avellino 1995, 1955

A causal conversation, a remembrance, in front of the rebuilt cathedral about a hired driver and the long ride into the city for the August *Festone,* the big feast . . . at Uncle Tobias' holiday dinner, they tried to serve my dad a chicken's head and neck bones. Then my father's tempered response that he didn't eat chicken heads and neck bones, and never would. These same relatives who borrowed 800,000 lire then pretended not to be home when, on another occasion, my father tried to collect the debt. Forty years later—not one lira paid back, not even a cup of coffee. It's no wonder my mom contends that Tobias' wife, Immaculata, died so young, barely fifty, of a heart attack.

Twenty-four hours after they buried Zia Immaculata, her body likely still cold from the ice they laid her on that rainy hot August day, passersby said they heard screams from the crypt where she lay. When the rain stopped and the ground stopped threatening to wash all the dead down the hill, it was said the cemetery groundskeepers opened Immaculata's coffin, only to find she had scratched her own face, in long, riverlike streaks of drying blood, from the sheer terror of realizing . . . she'd been buried alive. My narrator-parents relate this without the slightest touch of remorse, with that calm that comes from years of hard living. After all, it was people like her, who served chicken heads on feast days. *She got what she deserved.*

Orchiectomy

I. Delirium with Literary Antecedents, Eroticized

Whitmanesque, I hire myself to be his nurse,
        while sections of orange slowly disappear
                into the Cuisinart in the hospital's kitchen.
        A friend extracts me surgically from a chair

and waits until midnight, until the general anesthesia wears off,
        to help me walk him around the room.
                Instructions: stay awake, walk.
        The body is with the father, but the father

is not. . . . Instructions: take four Motrin tablets
        to equal prescription strength.
                Eyes without feeling, ears without hands.
        My mouth is full of bees and carbonated water;

the bees of mercy incise the air even as Elijah's fire
        consumes the wood, the stones, the dust,
                the water. The father's perkier now,
        he sits up in bed and flirts with the male nurses,

legs akimbo, he's a horseman—accustomed
        to riding over long stretches of terrain.
                [He] *bends, look. Back, elbow and liquid waist,*
        In him all quail to the wallowing o' the plough.

Instructions: don't retch. Retching is similar strain
        in terms of muscle involvement.
                At the follow-up appointment we learn the latest
        health tips though the wit's diseased and my back aches.

II. Meditation with Biblical Knives

For three days now I've slept on the floor at my in-laws',
       the Tens pack like bolts of lightning.
            The Prince of Judah was given nine and twenty knives:
       as incentive to build a temple in Jerusalem.

[God] *hath given all the kingdoms of the earth:*
       he hath charged others to build a house of clemency.
            I cannot discern the noise of the shout of joy
       from the noise of the weeping of the people.

In his purgation the father agrees to mutilate himself
       like the tribeless people of Israel
            who used knives and lancets
       till the blood gushed upon them.

Instructions: more fluid, rest, the flesh is
       revitalized by a new lexis of fire.
            And neither do thou anything to him,
       for now I know thou fearest God.

Instructions: use Vitamin E to prevent discoloration of skin;
       call a cab driver to help with the extra baggage;
            ask the parking authority for a temporary disability
                permit.
       Cleave the general ear, the air is eager.   **19**

Pleiades

Remember what the sky was like
that time sister ran away,
twilight approaching,
my unbuttoned shirt, the Buick
parked out front.
I sat in the street
by the corner curb writing
with chalky pieces of slate,
marking a line
for every secret she told,
for every furtive don't-tell-on-me-ok-baby look,
a line, for that bright orange minidress,
and her color-of-the-month curls,
a line for all the whispering and
the cars whisking by,
my knees covered in gravel; another
for all the times I sat in the back seat
and she was up front making love with whatever guy;
a line, for the police officer
patting my cheek, his stroking my hair
as if to say everything would be all right,
when he knew all along it wouldn't.
Her roots were starting to show.
And in tonight's wild constellation,
where I see a million
tiny flecks of light in the sky—
Cerberus barking, Hector abducted
across a wide dark river,
Helen calling out for him—
I think of her, my barely visible sister,
and wonder how she's doing out there
in Northridge, California,
with Frankie, her husband,
and their two cats.

Uncle Carmine

That morning, the phone

rang, Saturday,

mother answered,

barefoot

she stood

at the hallway phone, sobbing.

I tried to move her

to the bedroom,

but she wouldn't budge.

She called me Angeline,

my sister's name, and asked me

to investigate the draft

in the house. *Put cotton in*

the keyholes, if you have to.

She Speaks to Me from the Birthing Waters

My she-ghost is walking toward the Calvario again, up the curved end
of Via Nuova, where evening descends in curves.

At the end of the street, she stoops to pick up some imaginary fallen
      thing—
a blessing, an injured bird, used stamps.

And she keeps walking toward the woodcut effigy
of the Woodcutter Jesus, his weathered arms outstretched

toward the harvest's mechanical limbs. Several
now shake fig trees, olive trees, etc.;

and I smell that sharpened lemon smell.
Almonds too, uneaten, and strewn onto the dusty ground,

indecipherable in their tinny, resurrected language:
this Soil of Plenty, *Piano di Grazia*, disparaging fields.

In the burnt and stippled countryside, tractors
plow the earth, hungry for the remembered taste.

This land so close to the sea of silvered fish,
sardines in the sea grass, among cooling, stoppered bottles of wine.

Tonight she is my fastest ghost, mercury, my passion fruit,
in a perfectly struck pose.

And if she mutters to me, in her head-cocked, heavy fugitive tongue,
I will answer in a silence so forlorn, she would gladly surrender

her own lost voice. Tonight her message is written in the resistances
of our Southern Apennine village, at the limits of the mountain.

I want to write my love all over her, make up for lost time;
unwieldy arm cast, agonizing trophy case of scribbled promises.

I want to ship myself, 1972, a gnat-stained parcel, to that other country
she ran off to; her glance a mantel of violet-scented candles.

That child is electric in the indiscriminate weeds of her hips,
dandelions and chicory pour from her mouth—

balm for this child-toting specter of my sister, strange avenger, who forever
scrambles through the second-floor veranda of our house.

Beloved ghost, from this storybook's trapdoor, I am heavy
with semolina flour and the sweet forgiving sweat of you.

The Northern Savages—Notes and Index

Arthur's twelfth battle:

Hadrian's wall and garrisons
No longer bar
The lusty, the famishing barbarism

The lusty famishing barbarism
The Latin of Nennius
The Saxon pirates

Gildas the Wise
Bede the Venerable
Angles, Jutes and Saxons

Saxons as in saex
One-handed sword
Britain a refuge

Britain a refuge
Bede the Venerable
Seemed a refuge

The Saxons in the valley
The Battle of Mount Badon
Annals of Cambria

The King of North Wales
Name unpronounceable

In the contested land
Near Swindon, Liddington camp
Litter of imaginary remains

Swarm of:
569 or 570
The Welsh to the West

All that's left
Language unpronounceable
Chief Arthur

And his band
Of mail-clad cavalry

No Standing Still

At dinner,
we battle the dead,
spilling table wine
fearing the backhanded
slaps of callused hands.
Don't eat loudly.

The dead
are hungrier than ever
I feel them
whispering in my ear,
a trancelike litany
in another language:
"You stopped at the corner
on the way home, didn't
you; you ate the ends
off the bread."

I feel the dead
straddling me
trying to pin me down.

The buildings are moving.
My lips tear when they kiss my mouth.
My teeth ache.

I'm late
because I don't want to talk about death.
The dead are closer than ever
chasing me, following me
beneath my skin
peeling back—

At the Triple Treat Theatre

I used to pretend I stumbled into the place
casually, after a long day shopping or
I'd pretend I was a drunk
trying not to act drunk.

I'd catch my breath
and press against the door, waiting
for myself to stop teetering
then I'd browse through the porno magazines,
in quick impulsive start-and-stop motions
as if someone were ready to fight me
for the only item of its kind
still on sale.

But now, I strut into the place,
with my head up (as if I owned it)
and I do a beeline straight to the video booths.

All my worst nightmares have come true:
I have become that foul smelling
cubicle with the red light on.
And I dream I can hump as well
as anyone; and I dream
I can enjoy all that exciting humping.
And I dream that I hump for twenty-four hours,
(and it only costs 25 cents a minute).
I'm always humping, in the bed,
in the shower, in the jungle,
on the grass, on the floor.

And you know, I'm really starting to get tired.

When I try to change the channel
nothing comes on the screen clearly.
I think I'm a porn star and I feel
like a porn star, believe me.
But every porno star on this dirty
twelve-inch screen has lines through him,
and the vertical hold doesn't hold;
instead of that familiar grunting
and gasping, I hear static.
Everything is static.
And the twelve-inch video monitor,
in that dark booth, threatens to swallow
me whole, I am swallowed whole.

Now More Than Ever

There was a blue candle and
a white candle. There was a car,
a gift box, wrapping paper, and
a revolving platform. The rubbing
of his hands together spelled:
Clarity.

His arms around me
in the bed were seat belts.
The walking back and forth,
the ceaseless rocking, the can
of iced tea—too much left
unfinished.

The chart? Who could say
what exact measurements were necessary?
There was an adequate water cooler,
and water, right? That's important.
And earlier, when it was too early,

and we played tennis, he reminded me
of the trip. But if I were to travel
only to now, and if he were with me,
it would be enough.

July Fly Season

She only drank iced tea, never
the lemonade she'd make for me.
She never liked that sour lemon taste,
said it came over her "like the hives,
all blotchy and itchy-feeling,
seemed to take up all the air."

She was a sizable woman, and
in her prime men would snicker
and ask her, "How you holdin' up,
Ma'am?" "About as good as the chard;
picked three bushels full today.
Thank you very much."

July, fly season, and she liked
to sit outside on the screened porch
with the screen open, facing them,
one by one, swatting them,
with a flyswatter in one hand
and a Holiday Inn towel in the other.

"A man would never address a lady
in my day. But nowadays a repairman
will tell you he's been divorced, twice,
and I was just showin' him to the phone.
I'll tell you, ain't no such thing
as manners anymore . . .

"Now just pull those dark stems off,
so I can wash 'em in the tub,
and don't go splashin' around
and gettin' all wet and messy,
or your mother will give it to me
good, she finds out I had you workin'."

II.

The Rising

Occasionally
he washes up,

covered in seaweed.
And mother

wraps herself in
the shower curtain.

I'm in bed
with my sister,
comforting her.

Box of Broken Things

> . . . *tu ne vestisti queste misere carni, e tu le spoglia* . . .
> —Inferno, XXXIII: 61, 62

Place into it gently your anxiety over
surviving in spite of yourself, over
not returning to your hometown
to be buried. Place into it also your
remorse about beating us too often,
about fucking behind mother's back:
your forty-seven husbandless years,
the inability to act on your love
for other men. Place into it
the remorse you feel for fucking
your daughters, the hush money
you paid us not to tell how hard
you fucked us.

        Place into it
your sleepless nights, the nights
you wandered into the living room
to watch yourself fuck us
on the TV. Place yourself in
our shoes and forgive yourself
for eating from us a lifetime
of pleasures. Place yourself
at the dinner table like a place
setting that you tinkle against
your teeth; I'm the fork,
I'm the fork, my sister's a spoon.

Place yourself in your daughter's
shoes, the stilettos that pierce
the back of her children's heads.

Place yourself in your grandchildren's place and feel what it's like to be split up. Quarter yourself and feed yourself to yourself, on those nights you are hungry, feed yourself.

Poverty of Language

If a mother were to say: "I pray
to the Virgin you die of AIDS."

You see I'm doing it again,
shutting you out.

"I should have eaten *you* at birth."
This language is wealth,

a red dress,
an injection.

*

Father spoke to us
in erudite Italian:

pederasta—pederast,
infangare—to muddy,

to soil
as in ruining one's name.

Mother spoke
in a strange combination

of denial
and Southern Italian dialects:

femminiello,
she'd call me

femminiello,
she'd call my sister

femminiello,
my father

femminiello—one-half little girl,
one-half little faggot.

An Offering

Six hours across the ocean
he tiptoes straining to look
at Ghiberti's Baptistery doors . . .
all five feet five, one hundred twenty-eight
pounds; small Italian man with thinning
hair, large shellac-stained hands
in gluey dark blue work uniform,
his name neatly embroidered
in script on the front shirt pocket—

*

Go from your country and your kindred
to the land that I will show you. And I, a boy
of eight or nine, in a state of half-dream
half-nightmare followed him down carpeted steps
to a dank basement in America where musty air
surrounded us in a strange topography
of red velvet sofas, homemade wine vats,
an old stove where he stored tools,
and cracked boards whose paint peeled
away in tiny strips of transparent flakes.

When he allowed, I'd watch my father
master his trade in shadows to save a couple
of bucks on light bills—an impulse that led
to a fractured hip last winter when he slipped on ice
collecting cans for nickel refunds. I'd spend
hours there looking above at pine beams
stitch plumbing and wires to ceiling in neat
inverted pairs, until he, sawing, would call
me to hold the board steady. . . .

He said to hold tight, it won't hurt,
look away. Usually, I'd keep my eyes shut
or stare below at scarred pavement
filled with sawdust and wood shavings,
where cement hadn't set right—content,
when it was over, just to pull up
my pants and move aside. Effortlessly,
he repaired all the things of the world
and destroyed them.

Sacrifice of Isaac

Many nights, I am drawn to that area
of basement near his workstation.
To spite him, I flash lights on and off,
most times, until they blow out.
Or I piss in the flowerpots
or in his work boots, nearby.
Or I chip off pieces of better furniture
with a sharp stick.

Or I line up tennis balls on his workbench,
while judging my Miss Tennis Ball America Pageant—
bouncing, rolling, rating and finally
disqualifying some, but always leaving others
strewn about hoping he'll trip and fall.
I play through early morning, until I hear him
get out of bed or until light shines from that
two-foot window above the familiar worktable.

They taught us an angel called from heaven,
a ram was caught in a thicket by its horns.

The Way

The way of shepherds in the field,
   shepherds calling from the field.

The shearing of sheep, the midnight
   bleating. A wolf (but why?)
      cackling like a jackal.

The night of aluminum foil—
   of plastic wrap and handcuffs,
      lifting gloves and the smell of blood

pooling at our shoes. This lowering
   is how the end is. Counting. And this?
      A purple stain: stay with the image here—

stay with it. The garbage bags are piled
   higher on this street. They're named
      Mercy, Faith and *Desire.*

No one's sure of their order,
   how exactly they got here.

Iglesia Pentecostal de Dios, Manantial de Vida

The pendulous bob of the entire
left side of his hunched torso,
the clumsy placement of his crutch,
the way his wife trailed him
at a reverent, watchful distance,
a stripped-down procession of sorts
along the south sidewalk of 20th Street,
next door to the police station . . .
on another day, I could imagine her pinning money
on the raised saint during Holy Week,
impressed as I was by her steadfastness,
a Brueghel painting transformed
into this every-Sunday-evening parable—
how can I leave him, I imagine her
asking herself. I imagine also
a house filled with tall votive candles,
like the houses of absent fishermen
in Cavafy's poems, and the nephew
of my ninety-five-year-old landlady
rummaging through the trash, searching
for the broken-off hand of the statue
of Jesus of the Sacred Heart.
I imagine a man dancing
at the bar up the block
and all the hands that will reach
into his G-string; wonder
with whom he'll be going home later—
I pass this church every day,
have never actually been inside,
yet I imagine, distinctly, the processional couple
sitting in this storefront haven,
side by side, on collapsible metal chairs
listening to vociferous testimonies
nodding their heads in assent.

Prescription

You know this afternoon sun
and how sleep's relentless canyons
keep calling. Anxiety,
like a cold ocean of blue blood.
Won't anyone save me?

Any half-decent clothed man. Landscaper.
Mechanic? Veins heavy as water
pouring into the bath of the motel room next door;
outside, the thrum of a souped-up lowrider
along the highway. 4:31, 4:32—

the most menacing hour,
the pain of sciatica or a slipped disk,
shoulders stiffening.
Living with someone you do not love
is like a suicide watch,

only it's you you're watching,
the denouement of a murder mystery,
a severed and snakelike tongue,
an editor, St. Michael and the devil
stake-heart, cannibal.

The ideal apprentice demonstrates compassion,
I suppose: in the father country
a faggot could easily become a cause célèbre,
a reason for an anthology even,
even as the streets of Chelsea welter

with detail and IV bottles.
What a word "faggot" can be,
bundle of sticks, battle cry,
container and contained.
There's no part I want to liberate,

not that claptrap of bones, the taut skin
and especially that granite boulder who spawned me,
stolid and implicated, waving kitchen
utensils: a giant fly, hovering
above this sweetest earth.

Fairy-dust and rock, tongue-splitter and fire,
poison and syringe.

Cross-Country

Before my sister's divorce, I imagined driving her
back to her previous life, across Nevada, Arizona . . .

stopping alongside a dirt road near San Antonio,
on the way to the Mannerist Art Exhibition.

Because I want a redemptive art:
Pontormo's *Deposition* in Santa Felicità.

Because I understand how the Menendez brothers
must have felt, bullet holes of redemption;

and Susan Smith who made sure her boys
were securely strapped in seat belts before she drowned them—

Our own mother *would have eaten us at birth*
had she known how we'd turn out.

Give me Daniele da Volterra's *Crucifixion*,
anything by Bronzino, or Vasari—

I phoned my oldest sister this evening, the one father
couldn't get at when he lived away from us in Venezuela.

I wanted to tell her how this divorce was not news to me:
this was a clear case, with an antecedent.

I wanted to tell her clearly,
because we cannot always tell clearly.

I wanted to make her understand.
Because it's love we want.

His Touch

Today I learned the cost of living has not gone up.
I am not worth a three-percent raise.

Today I learned I can't live a day without
coming back to you, back to that point.

Not ten years of therapy, not an ocean
between us, a generation gap.

Today I learned the money I earn
will never be enough:

furniture polish, wax,
a spit-shine for all spit-shines.

How I have re-created those nights,
my first communion, my marriage;

and how I enjoy these reenactments,
lover-father, father-lover,

as much seducer as seduced,
as much only child as fatherless son.

And if I could carve myself
out of myself,

if I could bleed
a thousand baths—

because even then I'd repair myself
the way water does after it is entered.

Oh, the slippery friction of it,
the slippery fiction . . .

The Watch

We begin digging
at dusk, moist earth
thick with worms.

We begin digging
and continue
in spite of ourselves.

There are only men here,
walking, and I believe
in perfect submission.

Desire is good:
the primal burning
of bodies on land,

the movement of men
through foliage,
the thrashing.

It's the movement
that stirs me, not
the sound of water,

not the birds we hear;
no cries at all,
just the snap

of branches, the rustle
of low brush.
We undress—

if we lie perfectly still,
we may float
to the Boathouse

belly-up, across the lake;
a snag of branches.
My watch is gone.

It is right to praise God;
strip leaves off branches,
lay them atop bodies, burning.

This is desire:
the primal burning
of bodies on land,

the watching from water,
the swimming
and non-swimming,

the recollecting
and repetition,
the recollecting,

the repetition.

In the Garden

A spigot buried in,
in loosened earth, in a row
of bell peppers, zucchini.

Water trickling toward
our neighbor's yard
settles in, disappearing
as perspiration will.

He is clean-shaven today,
rested.

But his hands give him away,
every time.

III.

Premonition

I am entering the day: the asphalt opens up
replete with cobblestone—playing fields
instead of medieval alleyways. The elevated train's
Beaux Arts tassels crown the station as it slinks
corkscrew-like into the earth. On the ground

next to the entrance steps, a mangled teddy bear,
ursicide, we might call it, its woolen and sandy insides
snowbanking the curb. There's plenty of other
garbage, too: paper wrappers, glass, bottles
with their shard-edged metal tops still attached;

then the job, up the block. Longwood Avenue
in its eerie, alarm-clock light, suburban almost
until the Bruckner Expwy. snakes the landscape,
gray-black congested-road variety. Life Skills class
at the Treatment Center today, and J.'s sickness—

the call to the paramedics frightened all of us,
then his short-breathed, gurney-strapped ride.
It is almost dusk in another part of the world.
And these are the easy endings we hope for:
a cigarette break, a love letter for our lifetime.

Violence

—149th Street and 3rd Avenue in The Bronx

This thin line of despair that separates us today
from the rest of this community is a steam engine
in my veins, its whistle a muscle tightening
as we discuss the privilege that separates us from
the Dominican herbalist at the storefront *Botànica*.

In moments, we will enter a coffee shop
to order café *con muy poca leche* and imagine
(because this is what privileged minds do)
that the finely polished chrome bar and
its neatly clean tiled floor and yellow walls

will soon be completely splattered in blood.
We imagine, also, the mention of this incident
in a two-paragraph, 150-word-maximum story
written by some summer associate, to appear
on page three of the *NY Times* Metro section.

We will see a blurred picture alongside, with
a graffiti-filled gate, cordoned off by police tape
and this tell-no-tale scene: a pool of blood,
past the Café's entrance in which a Hispanic man's
body, barely distinguishable, will be sprawled,

his chin averted from the camera. At the end
of the article there will be mention of the religious
shrines inside the coffee shop, untouched
by the violence, how immaculately maintained
they are, adorned with new silk flowers—

the kind with plastic teardrops glued on.
There will also be mention of votive candles
that still shine brightly. We will muse over
these details, casually, as we walk to catch
the downtown "2," while I try hard to recruit

this privileged, overeducated white woman
to work for our community development agency
next door to the hottest crack spot in The Bronx—because
I believe in her liberal and complicated intentions,
and by now she feels guilty or convinced or both.

Clinic X

"I'm tired of some white asshole thinking
we need a savior, liberal bullshit.
This is my regime, and I got two,
maybe three years to turn this program around,
before I retire to Virginia.

If you give clients your phone number,
I'm comin' for you.

We don't need any of those dope fiend
dependency moves around here. My boss
is the only person who has my number
and if he calls at 11:00 P.M.
he *better* be paying half my rent.

Do you understand?
This is an interactive moment.

The moment has passed.

The reality is people want to be told
what to do. I'm sick of being some cruise director
on the Love Boat.

If I choose to spend my money on three
$5,000 mink coats, I do because I can.

Like I told that Save the Fur lady
those critters don't mean anything
to me *except* for their fur.
And if you try to spray-paint my coat,
I'm going to kick your ugly cracka' ass.

I know when to be nice to people.
But I'm comin' for you."

Schenectady

Next to the bank
   where they buy dust,

Main Street ends
   near the river at the crossroads

at the base of large, snow-capped mountains
   that rise from ash heaps . . .

Schenectady doesn't exist.

Schenectady is not glorious Ithaca.
   Even the name seems fake,

sounds like "skinny naked lady."
   The woman in the first part of the dream

is my grandmother.
   Her hands are bandaged.

Because she has no teeth,
   she speaks in the dialect of fish.

One by one she counts the street signs.
   There are seventeen:

Stop signs, U-turns,
   Railroad Crossings.

Wellington Diner Infidel

Easter morning, sitting in a beige vinyl seat.
I had just outed myself, distanced
Myself from so many things I wanted.

Cast away from the comforts of lamb shank
And relatives, my parents whispering
With the shame of me. Holy Week, and no one

To call family, not unholy, but reluctant,
Woozy as a newborn giraffe, crouched there
Beneath the knobby knees of its mother

Who's just delivered, from six feet above.
And each step, because in this life I'm born
Again, feels like a conversation in

A mysterious language. This new, stuttered
Existence, so far from the *Kyries*
And the thirteenth station in the church

Of my youth, named after St. Roch, healer,
Patron saint of the sick, especially
Revered in this Italian neighborhood

(Rocco, a name common as John.) It was
There that words first saved me, prayers to some
Sanctimonious muse. A surrogate

God-mother I spoke to again earlier
Today, when that familiar void overwhelmed me—
As it did that night on the edge of twenty

And suicide, when the parish priest,
Father Della Rosa, came to the house
And commanded in barely passable

English: "No matter what, God loves you."
Right about now in Rome, in the square
Of the saint I'm named after, namesake also

Of my grandfather, pilgrims begin to
Shuffle in—I can almost touch them through
The diner window—busloads full, from

Uganda, Brazil, Papua New Guinea.
Placards and whistles of tour guides excite
The air. Men, children, and mostly women

Crossing the threshold of the basilica,
The journey of a lifetime culminating
In this one rapturous moment. Some burst

Into tears, saving waters rushing over;
Others swoon, needing to be revived,
Slapped back—into this merciful life.

Dearest Evelyn, How Can I Make It Up to You?

Delicious creamsicle, I lost you on the way home.
I wanted to be first, spend our entire savings,
but the car wouldn't start; how I love French champagne!
That special code you taught me, I practice.

Fortunately, the seductive, tingling bells
led me across another endless field, another route.
No illicit lovelorn young thing,
no hotel in sight, in the wrong place.

What else could I do? Oh, to be two trains
traveling on the same track; the space between
two flowering trees and the only one
eating and playing stickball at the same time!

It was hot, the ball I hit kept rolling;
and her car was brand-new, foreign-made—
a speeding bullet without child-protective caps.
And I did that afternoon, all afternoon.

This candy heart I bought at the Hallmark Store.
It was good while it lasted.

No Apology

Half my age, a sapling practically, thriving
amidst the exhaust of cars, the onslaught of steady traffic.

This dogwood tree is an uncomplicated beauty;
intrepid from its circular, sidewalk cell,
flailing thin but abundant branches,

bud after bud opening its crossed whiteness
into a persistent drizzle on this evening of early dusk.

*

The dogwood's little-fisted worlds
announce the season with such understated vehemence,

like a street-corner missionary passing out his tracts.
But the tiny tree never exhorts us to repent!
And though the dogwood does not perfume the air,

nor offer any medicinal refuge,
it is nonetheless placid, steadfast.

*

Just last night, I returned, a prodigal and repentant lover,
offering a catalog of apologies and a fresh start.

How diffidently you linger above me,
pretending to avoid my head-on glances,
just out of reach, how forgiving!

Early Christian legend suggests the dogwood
is a zealous defender of faith and faithfulness—

*

but I want nothing half so exalted.
I would never deride a union so reciprocal
albeit functional and guarded.

And I pray if we should deceive each other again,
which in our elemental weaknesses is bound to happen,
that we will grant many such unexceptional encounters.

We don't always need praise;
our needs are not merely aesthetic.

*

But there is a certain way the shadows of this tree
lengthen into the busy street,
the way the rain bristles through branches . . .

Break

I overheard a man talking
about getting his chest waxed,
and all I could think about
was my friend Hollis going,
as she habitually does,
to Elizabeth Arden
for a complete makeover.

She's talking to me now
standing full length
in a full-length mirror.
I don't want to massage
her slender body,
she's not naked, and
I don't want her to be.

And I don't want her to leave the summer house—
I want her to stay here with me,
primping and fussing about herself.
I want the world to be as inconsequential
as our afternoons on the beach
where we couldn't hear ourselves
over the break of waves,

and where it didn't matter what we spoke about
or if we ever remembered our conversations.
But instead, I can hear her talking to me now:
"I don't want you to get sick,
I'll never judge you."
Hollis is brushing her hair back,
I can feel its thickness on my face.

Caught

Save me, O God, for the waters have come up to my neck.
                                                    —Psalm 69:1

On a recent afternoon I sat with my friend Barbara at the Joyce Theatre, watching David Parsons perform his now famous, signature dance piece, *Caught,* in front of a sold-out and enthusiastic house. Even after twenty years, David looks dapper as ever. In the lobby afterward, a crowd of children throngs around him, an incessant flash of cameras, his lanky frame elegant as ever in a gray crepe Armani suit.

Earlier we marveled at David's staggering energy—the breathtaking leaps—each thunderous clap of strobe light catching him in mid-flight: David flying, David dancing, David running through air, David parodying himself and, finally, David delivered by the hands of God to the foreground of the stage, right in front of us as the lights' rise, his chest heaving . . .

In 1982, when David Parsons first choreographed *Caught,* he couldn't have known; though all around him, in the dance world, the slow agonizing hush must have already begun: two principal dancers at Paul Taylor afflicted with a strange form of cancer, another at the Joffrey forced into early retirement because of constant bouts of flu. That same year, the *New York Times* ran a cover photograph of Martha Graham—much faded by age by then, funereal makeup and all—making a trip to St. Vincent's to visit a young dancer, dying suddenly of pneumonia.

Picture Window

Snow quietly fills our street, stillness
of a day off, drowsy morning of forgotten
alarms: by the time I wake, she will already
have taken her place, working, in front
of the picture window, unfazed, even today;
the white world rebuilding itself around her.

Beyond the wide-opened living room drapes,
a capricious shift of memories, soft piles
of white drifts: mother ironing, mother
threading a needle by the bright light.
This is no ordinary storm, but the sort
that recovers itself, that tempers even

the most destructive impulses by the process
of not remembering exactly. Mother is alone
on this particular morning; I have woken only
to her, nymph-like, industrious—a pungent
smell of cleaning solvents, and her explanation
that the tchotchkes that line the half-inch

ledge of the picture window have frozen
to the glass: frozen porcelain mice,
frozen Fabergé eggs, frozen earthenware.
How suddenly it seems our life together
has escaped from us so entirely, how we
have become tokens of our original selves.

And beneath the quietly falling snow,
spring's incorrigible blooms—azaleas,
rhododendron, the unwavering blue spruce,
the mimosa, dogwoods—seem impossibly
indistinct lumped together each against
the next, indiscriminate from the next.

Telling My Story

Last week at group I told them how pathetic we all are,
and a few of the guys remarked:
"What an interesting philosophical concept,"
even though I really meant how extra-pathetic
they are—one, a drug addict, another a sex addict,
another an alcoholic. And they told their stories
in such vivid detail; being cornered in the closet,
seduced (ridiculously) with Charms pops on the way home,
driven to the middle of the forest and buried
up to the neck, killing squirrels, etc.
You know, all the things some critics
would call pornographic.

But I'm in this stupid crisis therapy group, too,
and also pathetic by association, *"Dimmi con chi vai
e ti dirò chi sei!"*—Tell me with whom you go
and I'll tell you who you are, it would translate
(rather awkwardly) from mother's Italian dialect.
I can feel the lead rising in me, my liver
or some other vital organ weighing me down.

But I don't really want to talk about my story
so I tell them my theme song as a teenager was "Burning
Down the House," by The Talking Heads,
and they remind me how I'm the group clown,
how I have strong "avoidance tendencies."
So I respond by telling them, matter-of-factly, (and they don't flinch)
that my sister always wanted to sleep with me. She did so often,
on the daybed in the living room,
because she was scared, and I didn't know of what, until much later.

I tell them I remember my father calling my grandfather an animal,
telling how he used to get drunk and beat my grandmother
but nevertheless "managed to scrape by a decent living"
    (as a cobbler).

My father told one story, in particular, about killing grandfather's cat,
how he "snapped its neck" at the dinner table,
because he felt crazy, all the yelling
and drinking and wild cursing,
and he wanted to fight back for my grandmother's sake.

I remember feeling something close to sadness for my father,
wanting to do anything and everything he wanted
to make his pain go away. I was clear that he needed me,
that this wasn't a trick of seduction, but the way boys acted
if they wanted to grow into men.

I remember the worktable in the basement (most of the time)
and the wood oil and my pants
being down and my sister Angie staring from the bottom of the stairs
(once) into the darkness at the other end of the damp room.

Later, when we were much older, Angie told me (crying, hysterical, as
usual) that she knew what he was doing to me,
but she never did anything to protect me (as if she could)
because she was relieved he wasn't doing it to her anymore.

And I can't help feeling how lucky I am,
how much less pathetic, on the pathetic-continuum.
I'm not on drugs, not addicted to anything,
not fighting a custody battle.

And I realize when my father denies everything
and tells us he's a good father, he's partially right—
he fed us, he woke us for school
he sent us to good colleges, etc.

And still today in his especially pathetic way,
he tries to make it up to us
with money and trips (and we like that,
and worry about getting written out of his will).

In thinking about the group just now, telling this story,
I'm feeling it inside me, like a settling stomachache,
how nice it is to be sitting here listening to myself and six other men
talk about sexual abuse, as if we were at a poker game
or part of a sports team strategizing
about beating the next opponent.

And it all seems so ironic and out of context,
like a cheering crowd, all seven of us,
at a Cosmos soccer game in Giants Stadium in 1979.

Promised Land

All night in Tunisia lasted six hours
or twenty minutes, and Tunisia is not
the Middle East. Then Morocco,
unsafe there in Marrakech walking
through the market, being followed,
then chased, cornered.
How the dirt of this century fills
the ears. How the spiritual guide
spits the vitriolic words of blood.
Violence is androgynous, an old
man-woman with bright blond hair
and orthopedic shoes. Violence
doesn't wear makeup, not eyeliner,
especially. Egypt—scariest right now,
and possibly Israel, but not the hermetic
scriptural truth-seeking heretics
of the Apocryphal Books.
If it's true that air will become combustible,
that our lungs will eventually disintegrate
with each slight breath, let me die then
penniless somewhere
on the way to the Sea of Galilee,
penniless and gasping.

Medicine of Language

Shred the language, *dovrei scrivere,*
filter the commerce: *le strisce blu*
della copertina, concertina,
concentrate, this arduous excuse
to excuse all, why the past
is a mirror, in it an anorexic sister
hair falling, *capelli che cascano,*
cascare, cascade, a waterfall
hold up the building, a Mannerist
mantelpiece *pezzo di—pezzente*
peasant nothingness what you belong to
the dust of country, not even a country
a hill town in some vague Neopolis
metropolis, *non sono,* am not;
while he turns so quickly—
we all want to see a Ford Explorer
in the mirror, *nello specchio,* specter
the divided part, spectator
spectacolo, spectacular medicine

Lizard-Tree

Here in our garden you are
a gnarled, spindly intruder,
the transplanted heart
of an old conjure woman.

Nourishing you is no easy task:
the fastidious pruning
and insecticides, the plastic covers
for the cold. You ward me off

with claws three inches long
and shriveled fruit: poisonous
lemons whose fragrance
still haunts the yard.

How will I know you are dead—
when you no longer dart around me,
when the hiss of the wind subsides.

Tonight, the Survivor

Because I met the Raven on the street,
and because I knew the Raven before
he screamed into Hollywood self-
consciousness. Because I knew him
seven years earlier at the university
when he lived in a fifth-floor walk-up.
And because of the deadly sin of envy
and the river, I am saluting him
with *Veuve Clicquot,* gold label,
in his hotel room, at the Parker Meridien.

Because tonight I understand your accent,
its flexibility, the 18th, 25th, 23rd and 30th—
the frazzled ends of December. Thank you.
Because tonight I am no longer a fly
on the wall, a fly strip or the wallpaper,
not the floor mat, the dish towel, the hidden
secrets of the movie universe. Because
I have forgotten my ID card.
I am Saul and the grateful desert road.

Because of these things I can fish
for the payments, the return loan accounts.
Because I left my computer on.
Because I want to touch you. Tonight
I am the littlest rascal.
I need a lighter, a lighter I know
I will give back this time.
The yellow radio is on, on
the most comfortless night of the world.

Ice Lake

All day on the lake, the sun dismantling itself,
what to make of this darkening glittery pool, its diamond and
    resolute surface.
March, the gradual melting—
an old man ice fishing, his stalled truck at the lake's edge.
How soulless and solitary the corrugated tin and makeshift wooden
    shacks seem,
how they flourish in winter.

Imagine how frantically the ravenous fish poke at the fishing lines,
their luminescent bodies desperate for this dissident connection,
a four-inch layer of slush above them
on the thickly hardened ice.
Just now, the growing shadows quicken, two brightly dressed teens
stride assuredly across the shortcut of lake, toward North Hero.
The scene registers harsh light, atrophied muscles, snapping to
    attention.
How whole the earth seems: yielding, permeable.

As a child I believed pain was erasable. Someday, it would
    disappear, fall
from one sky to another, a continuous and invisible tumbling, like
    wind.
That's how I believed the world might end, the way ice melts,
    gradually at first,
then the aggressive breakage, piece by piece pulling against one
    another, eventually
surrendering to the force, flowing into it, then dissipating.
The wind remembers the undulant patch of gravel behind the
    cinder block garage, too,
and the desolate playing fields blanketed in snow—
I repeat these things, confidently, to myself.

Sometimes on the way home from work, late at night in the subway
    station,
an accordion and harmonica can sound like a finely rehearsed
    orchestra,
the kind I imagine in a smoky European cabaret.
That's why I am certain of almost nothing, sitting here, staring
across the lake's glistening surface—a closure that resists us,
this desire to blend into landscape.
How can we explain the pieces of detail, vanishing.

Peter Covino was born in Italy and educated there and in the States, where he earned an M.S. degree from Columbia School of Social Work; currently he is a Steffensen Cannon Fellow in the Ph.D. Program in English/Creative Writing at the University of Utah. Covino is also the author of *Straight Boyfriend*, winner of the 2001 Frank O'Hara Chapbook Prize; his poems have appeared in *Colorado Review, Columbia, The Journal, The Paris Review, Verse,* and *The Penguin Book of Italian American Writing,* among other publications. He is one of the founding editors of *Barrow Street* and Barrow Street Press.

New Issues Poetry & Prose

Editor, Herbert Scott

Vito Aiuto, *Self-Portrait as Jerry Quarry*
James Armstrong, *Monument in a Summer Hat*
Claire Bateman, *Clumsy*
Maria Beig, *Hermine: An Animal Life* (fiction)
Kevin Boyle, *A Home for Wayward Girls*
Michael Burkard, *Pennsylvania Collection Agency*
Christopher Bursk, *Ovid at Fifteen*
Anthony Butts, *Fifth Season*
Anthony Butts, *Little Low Heaven*
Kevin Cantwell, *Something Black in the Green Part of Your Eye*
Gladys Cardiff, *A Bare Unpainted Table*
Kevin Clark, *In the Evening of No Warning*
Cynie Cory, *American Girl*
Peter Covino, *Cut Off the Ears of Winter*
Jim Daniels, *Night with Drive-By Shooting Stars*
Joseph Featherstone, *Brace's Cove*
Lisa Fishman, *The Deep Heart's Core Is a Suitcase*
Robert Grunst, *The Smallest Bird in North America*
Paul Guest, *The Resurrection of the Body and the Ruin of the World*
Robert Haight, *Emergences and Spinner Falls*
Mark Halperin, *Time as Distance*
Myronn Hardy, *Approaching the Center*
Brian Henry, *Graft*
Edward Haworth Hoeppner, *Rain Through High Windows*
Cynthia Hogue, *Flux*
Christine Hume, *Alaskaphrenia*
Janet Kauffman, *Rot* (fiction)
Josie Kearns, *New Numbers*
David Keplinger, *The Clearing*
Maurice Kilwein Guevara, *Autobiography of So-and-So: Poems in Prose*
Ruth Ellen Kocher, *When the Moon Knows You're Wandering*
Ruth Ellen Kocher, *One Girl Babylon*

Gerry LaFemina, *Window Facing Winter*

Steve Langan, *Freezing*

Lance Larsen, *Erasable Walls*

David Dodd Lee, *Abrupt Rural*

David Dodd Lee, *Downsides of Fish Culture*

M.L. Liebler, *The Moon a Box*

Deanne Lundin, *The Ginseng Hunter's Notebook*

Barbara Maloutas, *In a Combination of Practices*

Joy Manesiotis, *They Sing to Her Bones*

Sarah Mangold, *Household Mechanics*

Gail Martin, *The Hourglass Heart*

David Marlatt, *A Hog Slaughtering Woman*

Louise Mathias, *Lark Apprentice*

Gretchen Mattox, *Buddha Box*

Gretchen Mattox, *Goodnight Architecture*

Paula McLain, *Less of Her*

Sarah Messer, *Bandit Letters*

Malena Mörling, *Ocean Avenue*

Julie Moulds, *The Woman with a Cubed Head*

Gerald Murnane, *The Plains* (fiction)

Marsha de la O, *Black Hope*

C. Mikal Oness, *Water Becomes Bone*

Bradley Paul, *The Obvious*

Elizabeth Powell, *The Republic of Self*

Margaret Rabb, *Granite Dives*

Rebecca Reynolds, *Daughter of the Hangnail*

Rebecca Reynolds, *The Bovine Two-Step*

Martha Rhodes, *Perfect Disappearance*

Beth Roberts, *Brief Moral History in Blue*

John Rybicki, *Traveling at High Speeds* (expanded second edition)

Mary Ann Samyn, *Inside the Yellow Dress*

Mary Ann Samyn, *Purr*

Ever Saskya, *The Porch is a Journey Different From the House*

Mark Scott, *Tactile Values*

Hugh Seidman, *Somebody Stand Up and Sing*

Martha Serpas, *Côte Blanche*

Diane Seuss-Brakeman, *It Blows You Hollow*